Does Freed[om Mean]
You're Free?

From Prison to the Palace

The Story of
Gene Porter

Publisher: Natacha Williams
Execute the vision ghostwriting and publishing services.

ISBN: 9798332429781

Cited from "The King Crawley Podcast"

Does freedom Mean You're Free Poem?

You convicted me of a crime that all the evidence said I did not commit
You gave me fifty years and suspended twenty-five of it
No prom, no graduation, and no way to learn.
Took my name and gave me a number to learn
You denied my appeals and all my request to be set free I yelled in silence " It was not me"
I carried the time to the door stood 10 toes down on that concrete floor
In the back of my head Frank Sinatra song would play because I walked through prison and I did it my way
Even though I'm free I carry the burden of being a felon to this day.....
Does Freedom Really Mean You're Free.....

-Gene Porter

Who is Gene Porter A.K.A Smokie?

Gene Porter was born in Cincinnati Ohio, to Vanessa Reese and Gene Porter. He was born in March of 1976 and he was the second oldest of five children of the four that are still living. Gene lost his brother, Gary, when he was a toddler. When he was 12 years old, his mom moved to Virginia with a childhood boyfriend of hers. Gene also has an older brother, Jamie, who his mom had put up for adoption due to her mother because of her age. Vanessa did her best to raise her son, Gene, with the proper tools to get through life despite her having a troubled childhood herself. Eugene aka Smokie, named after Smoking Joe Frazier, was the oldest of the rest of his siblings, Gary, Tamika, and Nicole.

Dedication

First, I would like to dedicate this book to my baby sister, Nichole Reese, for making trips up and down the highway to visit me when I was in prison. Once she turned 18 years old, she started visiting me until my release day.

I would also like to dedicate this book to my sister, Ta'mika, for her silent prayers for me and to my extended family, The ones that are watching over me from heaven-Mook, Dre and Mama Shirley.

Introduction

WOW, 17 years old and facing time in prison for a murder you did not commit. This is the story of so many of our young Black men growing up in the streets and trying to survive. Some of them because this is what they had to do and some because it was something to do. Eugene "GENE" Porter, Jr. was one of our young Black men, who got caught up in the streets and yes, he did things he was not supposed to do but, murdering someone was not his crime.

Go on this journey of a young black 17-year-old male who was at the wrong place at the wrong time and ended up in prison for a murder that he did not commit. Gene's story is a story that we hear too often. Gene was convicted and sentenced to 50 years with twenty-five suspended and served 18 years before being released in 2012.

His story is so powerful, being 17 years old, still a youth, and had to go through serving time for a murder that he did not commit and a young Black man at that. His transparency, strength, and tenacity are so touching. He is into fitness and now has a gym in Emporia, giving back to his community, going into the schools and the prisons sharing his story, and not letting what he has been through define the man that he was destined to be. Things happen for a reason, whatever that may be and what doesn't kill us truly makes us stronger even though no one should ever have to experience something like this. He is truly the epitome of strength.

-Natacha Williams,
Ghostwriter & Publisher.

Forewords

At the time of writing this, I've known Gene for about 10-11 years. I crossed paths with him during a rough patch in my life. I used to hit the gym over on South Main Street in Emporia, and one Sunday, I spotted this new guy there.

    We exchanged nods, making the usual gym small talk. Then came this moment when I was struggling with a shoulder exercise, and Gene stepped in. He showed me a shoulder movement of which I had never even thought. That single act hinted at something special about him.

    As we got talking more, he opened about his journey, including his recent return from an 18-year stint in prison for a crime he didn't commit. During our conversation, I had to pause and ensure I wouldn't offend with my next words.

But I told him straight: if he had not mentioned his time behind bars, I wouldn't have guessed that he spent 18 years in prison.

Now, don't get me wrong—it's not meant as an insult or anything. But when you have folks close to you who have been through the system, you tend to notice certain signs and mannerisms. Yet, with Gene, none of that was apparent.

Over time, Gene has proven himself as a consistent friend—not the type who measures friendship by material things but by principals Principles and codes that too many nowadays seem to forget. He has shown himself to be trustworthy in countless situations both inside and outside the walls. I have witnessed numerous victories, big and small, from the sidelines or right in the thick of it with Gene.

So, I will not dive into the specifics of his story here. Just know this: if Eugene Porter can weather the storms he has faced and continues to face, then I hope his journey inspires you to keep pushing forward. Because when you see what he has overcome, you realize that anything is possible. - **King Crawley**

It was such a pleasure learning more about Eugene Porter, "Smokey" is what his close friends and family calls him. I had the privilege of speaking to Cornelius Turner, another man wrongly convicted of a crime that he did not commit and that is how he met Mr. Porter when they were in prison together.

So, this is what Mr. Turner had to say. Smokey was a quiet guy, he was never into penitentiary things so to speak, like gambling, basketball, card games, those type things he wasn't into that, he was into working out all the time, working out and working out all the time, he was just a good guy and I don't remember how we met but, I know someone how we both started talking about our cases and the fact that we were both innocent. I was telling Smokey just the other day that the hardest part about being in prison and your innocence is, a lot of people think that they are not guilty but they are not innocent. The hard part is that you have the people in there know they did it but still claim to be innocent. So, the perception is that everyone thinks they are innocent and you must deal with that perception of you knowing you are innocent and not knowing when you will get to go home.

SN: Mr. Turner, said that he was hopeful at one point about his case and they were going to realize they made a mistake and he was going to get to go home and that time of him being proven innocent never came for him as well as Mr. Porter, even though they were.

Smokey and I knew that eventually they would realize that they made a mistake by locking them up and that day was going to come and they would get to go home. But, with Smokey they locked a guy up in his case but the guy lied and said it was Smokey. Smokey was an all-around good guy to the point when we were like 23 or 24 years old, I let Smokey write to my sister and I did not let anyone mess with my sister. With his character and nature, I did not have a problem with him writing to my sister. Also, I knew when he got home, he would do fitness, there was no doubt about it. In conclusion, after MR. Turner and my conversation, he sent me a text to sum it up on the character of Mr. Porter.

Smoke, what can I say? He is an exceptional friend who I genuinely believe was wrongly convicted. I've had the privilege of knowing Smoke (Gene) since 1994 or 1995 and I can confidently attest to his outstanding character and kindness. Despite the challenges he faced in prison, Smoke has always been dedicated, consistently demonstrating a remarkable ability to empathize and support those in need. -**Cornelius Turner**

The case information: Eugene Arthur Porter, Jr. (appellant) appeals from his bench trial first-degree murder conviction by the Circuit Court of the City of Hopewell (trial court). The appellant contends that the trial court lacked jurisdiction over him because in a transfer hearing held in the Juvenile and Domestic Relations District Court (J&D court) the detention order recited that: The Court finds that the evidence presented at the transfer hearing was insufficient to establish probable cause to believe that the juvenile committed the alleged delinquent act, and therefore the case is retained in this Court for trial at a later date.1

For the reasons that follow, we affirm.
1 The order further directed that the appellant "be detained in an appropriate secure juvenile detention facility."

The record discloses the following procedures and findings: December 15, 1993, a petition was issued in the J&D court against the appellant, then seventeen years old, charging him with murder. On December 17, 1993, pursuant to Code § 16.1-269 (since repealed), the Commonwealth moved to transfer the case to the circuit court for the trial of the appellant as an adult. A transfer hearing was held in the J&D court on February 4, 1994. That court denied the Commonwealth's motion, finding that "the evidence presented at the transfer hearing was insufficient to establish probable cause to believe that the juvenile committed the alleged delinquent act, and therefore, the case is retained in this Court for trial at a later date." On February 25, 1994, the Commonwealth, pursuant to former

Code § 16.1-269(E), filed a notice of removal in the circuit court.

On April 13, 1994, the appellant filed a motion to dismiss in response to the Commonwealth's notice of removal, claiming that the circuit court lacked jurisdiction (1) "to review the issue of transfer since no decision on such issue was made by [the J&D court]" and (2) "to determine the issue of probable cause since such determination lies within the exclusive original jurisdiction of the appropriate [J&D] court." After a hearing on the Commonwealth's motion to remove the case and upon appellant's motion to dismiss the proceedings, the circuit court held that the requirements of former Code § 16.1-269(E) had been satisfied and authorized the Commonwealth to seek an indictment against the appellant.

On April 20, 1994, appellant was indicted for murder. On July 29, 1994, the appellant applied for a writ of prohibition with this Court alleging that the circuit court lacked jurisdiction to permit the Commonwealth to seek an indictment because the J&D court had failed to find probable cause. This Court denied the application, stating that "the relief sought [was] not cognizable for review by a petition for writ of prohibition."

On November 9, 1994, the appellant was tried and convicted. The issue the appellant raises on appeal is not entirely consistent with the finding of the J&D court. The hearing held in that court was a transfer hearing, not a preliminary hearing to determine probable cause of guilt. Former Code § 16.1-269 provided a vehicle by which the J&D court may hold a hearing for the sole purpose of determining whether a juvenile charged with a crime should be retained in the J&D court for trial or transferred to the circuit court for criminal proceedings as if the juvenile were an adult. That vehicle was appropriately referred to as a "transfer hearing," and the finding did not determine guilt or innocence, only whether the case should be transferred to the circuit court or retained in the J&D court for trial.

When the J&D court denied the motion to transfer and ordered that the juvenile's case be retained in that court, subsection (E) of former Code § 16.1-269 provided the Commonwealth with a review method by the circuit court of the J&D court's decision. That subsection provided that in such cases when the attorney for the Commonwealth "deems it to be in the public interest," the Commonwealth may seek a removal of the case to the proper circuit court. After notice as provided in former Code § 16.1-269(E), the circuit court must then within a reasonable period after receipt of the case from the juvenile court, (i) examine all such papers, reports, and orders and (ii) conduct a hearing to take further evidence on the issue of transfer, to determine if there has been compliance with this section, but without redetermining whether the juvenile court had sufficient evidence to find probable cause, and enter an order either remanding the case to the juvenile court or advising the attorney for the Commonwealth that he may seek an indictment. The record before us discloses that the transfer hearing and review thereof were conducted in accordance with the requirements of former Code § 16.1-269. The issue as stated by the appellant fails to recognize that the hearing in the J&D court was to determine whether a transfer of the case should be made. The J&D court ruled that the case should be retained. While the J&D court cited a lack of "probable cause" as the basis for denying the Commonwealth's motion to transfer the appellant's case, the record makes clear that the J&D court concluded that the Commonwealth had failed to demonstrate probable cause or cause to justify a transfer under former Code § 16.1-269. If the J&D court had found probable cause lacking against the appellant, it would not have retained the case for trial later; rather, it would have dismissed the charge against the appellant outright. Whether proper procedure was followed in transferring the case to the circuit court, no constitutional or statutory right has been abridged. The appellant was accorded all rights and protections required by law. For the reasons stated, the judgment of the trial court is affirmed.

How It All Started

Most people call me Strong Temple; and some know me as Uncle Gene, or Personal trainer of Emporia. I am originally from Cincinnati, Ohio. I moved to Virginia in the summer of 1988, and what I discovered put me in a predicament and lifestyle that ended up costing me 18 years in prison for a murder I did not commit!

The issue stems from my lack of listening skills and stubborn nature. I didn't follow my mother's instructions. I ran the streets even though I didn't have to. I was receiving allowances and performing my chores, but these tasks lacked excitement. After moving to the southside of Richmond, Virginia, and observing the differences in wealth, black legends, and other aspects of life, I felt a strong desire to join the flashy lifestyle because of the money and girls. This led me to work on the streets for someone, but I have always prioritized protecting my family more than anything else. I have always been the kind of person who, when faced with a challenge, would act when necessary. My mother instilled in me the value of not being a follower but also leading others in the neighborhood. That's exactly what happened; I found myself drawn to the crack game. Working for someone who introduced me to the crack game, which ultimately led me to decide not to work for anyone else. At the end of the day, the percentages of 70-30's or 60-40's didn't seem correct, and the breakdown of the money didn't make sense, so I had to leave. I decided to start my own operation. Being on the streets and constantly receiving calls for assistance marked the beginning of my journey. I didn't even understand the concept of fearlessness, nor did I know what fear meant. I was 12 or 13 years old. I had lost the ability to cope with fear. Bullying was something I witnessed firsthand, as well as something I experienced myself. Despite being bullied, I emerged as a fighter. I came from a background of people who were professional boxers, demonstrating a strong understanding of self-defense. I started defending myself. I started establishing a reputation, and people always gravitated towards me; they would say things like, "Go get them smoky." I'm fighting on behalf of the other people because they know I'm going to show up. When I arrived, all communication between anyone and my family ceased. If you were a resident of Petersburg or Hopewell, you were likely familiar with the Pettaway, Monroe, and Taylor families. It was always a given that these were the people who would fight quickly and get into trouble. I was living in Norfolk but I used to visit my family in Hopewell, but because I usually got in trouble, my probation officer advised me not to return and to stay away. But that's my family, so I'm thinking I want to go back and visit them. Is it right to go there? But you will see, because of this visit, my whole life changed.

   I wanted to visit my family because I haven't seen them in a while. That day my mom was leaving for work and she instructed me to stay in the house until she returned. Stay here with your sister until I return. I'm going to see my neighborhood. I haven't been in the Petersburg area for, like, three years. My plan was to pop in, and then slide right back out. But I ended up staying longer because of the holidays and other circumstances. It was around Thanksgiving time, and I had gotten up that morning wanting to see, you know, at that time we had like stepbrothers and sisters. So, whoever your mom or dad was with, their kids were considered your stepsisters and stepbrothers. So, I went to my stepbrother and sister's house, after my mom instructed me not to. As I strolled down the street, I caught sight of the man who would be the one to deceive me. His brother and I used to be cool. His nickname was Kluck. So, as I and Russell, my stepbrother, were exiting the Five Forks store I looked to the right and saw Shawn standing near the telephone booth, so I walked over there and asked him where everybody was hanging out. He informed me that everyone was hanging at the heights, and then he received a page. We did not have cell phones back then, but we had beepers, and when he gets a page, he goes to the telephone to call the number that came up on the pager. I overheard him conversing with the individual, during which he mentioned his location would be at the Breeze Inn. After he hung up the phone, he said, "Smoke man, I need to leave." Without giving it any thought, me and Russell began walking down the street. I returned to my fam house later, around 1 p.m. in the afternoon, due to the events that had transpired earlier in the day. So, I am walking back down the street with my cousin Emanuel. We met Tony aka Bone at the corner. We saw everybody standing outside this lady's (she's one of my distant cousins) house, and we heard Shawn talking about something that had happened and I heard him say, "He got shot." and I still harbor a deep connection to that neighborhood because I have a connection. I am prepared to go, assuming it's someone from our community or someone I grew up with. He repeatedly claimed to have been shot, to which I responded, "Who got shot, Shawn?" He responded, "Smokie, you don't know him." So, I just leaned back on the car as he was telling the story. He was like, the guy who came from around the building shot Danny in the head. He claimed that he managed to catch him just as he was about to fall to the ground, and laid him down. Then he said, "The guy went away, came right back, and shot Danny in the body." So, at the time he said it, he took the stuff off him and showed us what he had. Thus, his possessions included money, crack, and the man's beeper. So, I leaned back on the car. While they were telling everyone who was out there, I realized that one of the witnesses, a girl nicknamed Wormy, was also present, along with her mother. So, I am saying if Wormy and him were out there, they would tell what they saw. Therefore, Shawn handed the drugs to his cousin, who then proceeded to hide them around the house. So, I did not think anything else of it, so I left and went on with the rest of my vacation. I didn't give it any further thought, even though I was still on probation at the time. Back in Norfolk, I checked in and was asked about the situation.

Wait, let me rewind. So, before I left, I was in the barbershop here, and people were talking to the barbershop. You know, everything is talked about in the barbershop. So, I heard people in the barbershop saying that Shawn killed the man, so I am like a man thinking about it. They are about to get Shawn. I thought to myself, "Man, they're about to punish Bro for something he didn't even do." As I was leaving the barbershop, I spotted one of our neighborhood guys, and I asked him, "Have you seen Shawn?" He said, "Yeah, he's down in the country." He was in Prince George, and I thought, "People in the barbershop were saying, 'He killed that man; he needs to go tell them that he didn't do it.'" But little did I know that the tables were going to turn.

So, I left and returned to Norfolk to visit my PO, who asked me, "What happened down there?" I was like, I heard somebody get killed. I had nothing to do with it. I am not responsible for any of this. A week has passed, and I am unsure if the probation officer has checked in with the city of Hopewell. Initially, when the police visited me, they simply asked me a series of questions. They were questioning me about what had happened and whether Shawn was responsible. Now, during our conversation, it came to my attention that Shawn was with someone else. So, I said, "No, but I don't know about the other guy he was with, because I am not even familiar with him." They left, but not before asking if they could take a picture of me. I was wearing the starter jacket, but it wasn't my own; it belonged to one of my friends. Do you know how back in the day we used to trade starter team jackets and clothes with your boys, and I was in Nas error, so the guy had my army jacket while his starter jacket? Then they attempted to take a picture of me, to which I initially objected. However, they later said, "You don't make us come all the way back here to take a picture of you." Therefore, I accepted the situation, knowing that I had done nothing wrong. They took a picture of me with the jacket on, and then they left. Two weeks later, they came back and said, Mr. Porter, you are under arrest for the murder of Danny McClure. That incident changed my whole world. I began to question whether it was a mistake, as I didn't fully comprehend or understand the situation at first.

At that time, I still had faith in the justice system, and for every charge I ever had, I pleaded guilty too. So, I'm thinking to myself, "This must be a misunderstanding because I know I didn't have a gun, I know I didn't kill that man, I never saw that man, and I never had a motive to kill that man." Therefore, they requested permission to inspect the house and collect some property. They proceeded to gather the starter jacket, some shoes, and any other necessary items to assess for gunpowder residue. That night, as we rode back to Hopewell from Norfolk in the pouring rain, I fell asleep. I heard the officer ask me if I was sleeping, and I jumped up, saying, "No, because I don't know what's going on at this time." Do I fall asleep? What plans do you have for me? All of this occurred prior to the police killing us; we were dealing with some issues at that time.

When I arrived at Crater Detention Hall for another shift, I was still considered a minor due to my age of seventeen. When I arrived at the detention center, after undergoing a mandatory shower, they placed me in a jumpsuit and led me down the hallway. As I walked down the hall, I noticed that there were approximately twenty-three cells. I'm going in the boy's wing. As we are going down the hall, there are people banging on the doors, and they are hollering, "The guy is in here that killed Danny." "The guy who killed Danny is here."

Despite having many friends in Petersburg, I was still associated with Hopewell, even though Danny was from Petersburg. My family is from Hopewell, but everyone I miss, including my team, is from Petersburg. My neighborhood never held me back, as I found acceptance everywhere I ventured. They kept saying, "The guy is in here who killed Danny," and they were like, "Yeah, we're going to get him tomorrow morning," so I knew how it went because I had been to the Crater before." It's a fight, so I know what it is. If you have certain charges and you hurt someone's family member and you don't know who is related to who, a fight is going to happen.

So, I slept light, and still, I don't even think I cried; it's just a misunderstanding, and it's going to be over soon, I thought to myself. That morning, because I was positioned at the back, they allowed me to exit first. So, after they let me out first, I was able to go to the TV room first. Once I reached the TV room, I strategically positioned my chair to observe everyone exiting the hallway. If they want to start a fight with me, I want them to be in front of me, not behind me. Even if they do and I fall and they stomp on me, kick me, or do anything else, I will remain strong! So, as people started coming down the hall (I had a slight reputation), everyone was like, "Smoke, what are you doing here?" Smoke, what are you doing back in Hopewell? So, I was like, Dude, they said I killed somebody. They said I killed somebody by the name of Danny. Immediately, the men became enraged as they discovered that Shawn, the individual who had deceived me, had recently relocated to Richmond earlier that morning. Shawn was already in detention when his transfer occurred that morning. So, if they had known that Shawn had lied, they would have gotten him. So, they were like, "Shawn lied on you, and that's why they moved him." So, I was like, I still cannot believe that Shawnn did that to me. I did not believe it until pretrial, when Shawn stood up there and testified against me. He stood up and looked those people in the eye, lied, and said I killed Danny. What was so crazy was the conversation I had with the court-appointed lawyer the week before.

SN: When you are in those streets and know you are doing something wrong, make sure you have a lawyer. Not court-appointed, and/or make sure you know the law yourself. When I went to prison, I had to learn what they could say and do to me. Make sure you know, because we are the only people—Black people—who don't study the game and what we need to know. We learn about the game as we go!

So, I'm in there talking to my lawyer, Ray Lupold, who was my lawyer at the time and a court-appointed lawyer. He worked for Marks and Harrison. I thought I had a good lawyer (he is a judge now.) So, I asked him what was going to happen, and he said, well, you go to the pretrial; the pre-tail is to see if they have enough evidence to convict you of this. This was the highest charge or case I ever had—murder—and I did not know anything about pre-trial and all that stuff. So, the night before we were supposed to go to court, Tony ended up getting locked up. So, they were getting Tony off the streets so he wouldn't retaliate over someone burning down his house. Someone threw a fire cocktail and burned his house down. Tony was the one who was with me walking on the day of the murder. So, when Tony showed up in detention, I was like, OK, I got a witness that knew that I didn't do this, and he was out there with me when Shawn was telling the story. When we get to the holding tank, we are sitting there handcuffed to the chair, and at this stage, we are still juveniles. Do they bring us in differently from the adults? But in the adult-holding cell, Lamont Parsley is there. Lamont was also out there when Shawn was telling the story. Lamont looked at me and said, "Smoke, what are you doing here?" I was like, man. Shawn said that I killed somebody—that I killed that man. Lamont was like, Naw man, that's some bull.

So, we went to the pretrial, and they asked Shawn, the witness, what happened. Shawn says that I had a hoody on and he could only see part of my face, but he recognized my voice because we had been in detention together and he used my real name. The thing about when I was in the streets was that the only people who knew my real name were family or we went to school together because the teacher had to call out your real name, but to everyone else, I was Smoke. So, when he said my real name, that threw me off because he shouldn't know my real name. I know we have been in detention together, but he doesn't know me like that. Saying my name like we are familiar with each other.

When he started telling the story about the fact that, you know, he was behind the Breeze Inn, and I came from behind the back of the building, the way he told the story was that Shawn was standing on one side, Danny was in the middle, and Norris was on the other side, and he said I came up to him and said, "Do you have a problem with me?" He said, and then I shot Danny. So, basically, he said I walked up during them three talking, interrupted them to ask Danny, do he have a problem with me, and he said, I shot Danny in his torso, then he said Danny fell, and I walked away so many feet, and then I came back and then shot him in the head. Also, he said that he never saw the gun; he said I had the gun up in the sleeve of the jacket. So, as I'm sitting here listening to his story, I'm saying to myself, "He's lying; what do I do?" So, after that, they asked us to make our defense. What do you have to say? So, I tapped my lawyer on the shoulder, and I told him to call Lamont. Lamont Parsley and Tony Thomas who were in the back; they got locked up for something. I said to call them from the back, and my lawyer said, "Do you want me to go back there and talk to them?" I said no because I know they are going to tell the same story that we were all out there when Shawn was telling what happened. I want them to come out and tell what they know in front of everybody. So, they called Tony out, and they started questioning Tony about him knowing me; they asked him, "Do you know Mr. Porter? and Tony was like, "Who Smokey?" He was like,

Yeah, ever since Smokey moved to Virginia, we all hung around each other. Then they asked him, "Do you know Shawn Coleman? He was like, Yeah, Shawn and I are supposed to be cousins, and the man questioning him was like, "Ok, do you know anything about the shooting and what happened? He was like, we were all out on the heights when Shawn told us what happened, and me and Smoke walked to the corner together. Shawn was telling everyone about what happened. The lawyer that was questioning Tony said thank you, sent him to the back, and called for Lamont. He asked Lamont the exact same questions: do you know Mr. Porter, and he was like, yea; I know Smoke, and he asked, did he know Shawn, and Lamont was like, yea? I know, Shawn, we will all be in the neighborhood together; he said we were all out there when Shawn was telling the story. So, do you mean that Shawn knows who Mr. Porter is? He was like, Yeah, he knows Smoke. So, he was like, alright. The judge called for Shawn to come back into the courtroom, and the judge asked Shawn if he knew Tony Thomas. He said, Naw, the judge was like, you don't know him, and he was like, no, I don't know him. Then he said, "Do you know Lamont Parsley?" He was like, I know him from around the neighborhood, but I don't know him like that. So, the judge said, okay, you can leave. He sent Shawn back out of the courtroom, and I know people were like, why would Shawn lie about you? Shawn was being charged with robbery and murder; they were just charging me with murder.

The other part of this is that Shawn kept calling the guy—what I learned from the guy's family Shawn kept calling the guy all that morning, trying to get him to meet him somewhere. I kept saying to the guy, I've been trying to call you all day. Can you meet me at the gas station or at Exxon? And then, when the guy finally decides to meet, he gets killed. Either it was a set-up or something.

So, the judge sent Shawn out and told them to move him because he kept peeking in the door, and the judge was like, move him and stop peeking in the door. Judge Sam Cambell was the juvenile judge at the time, and he said everything that Shawn Cox is saying is a lie; he said Mr. Porter didn't kill that man. So, at that time, I was sitting there, thinking that I was about to go home. The first time I ever heard of your honor, I appealed. The prosecutor appealed and sent me upstairs to the high court. So, now my lawyer is asking, can I go back home to Norfolk or can he stay out here with my mom? The judge was like, ummmmm (they felt like Shawn was more of a threat to me than I was to him). Let's keep him in detention for his own protection. So, they believe downstairs that Shawn was the one who did it. So, they appealed it, and I stayed in jail. Now I have been given two court-appointed lawyers and an investigator. Now we are going back and forth with a lie detector test, and the police keep trying to get me to say something, and I keep saying that I didn't do this. The lawyer comes in when they decide to send me up to determine whether we have a judge or jury. The lawyer scared me because he is telling a young, 17-year-old Black guy that it's going to be all white people on the jury. At this time, I'm scared, so I told him I want a judge because I'm thinking I have it good with judges because I always plead guilty to my crimes.

Taking a judge case was the worst thing that I ever could have done because I didn't know about a jury of your peers, that you have twelve people you must convince, not just one person deciding your fate, and the police were still trying to get me to say something! They were asking me to give them something, like where the gun was. At first I thought about it because I know where some are at." "Like, naw, I didn't do anything. It was detective Rose Camacho and police officer Whittingham on the case. Camacho always used to tell me, "You didn't do this, Gene." We know you did not do it, and we know Shawn had something to do with it. They know that there is reasonable doubt, and it does not translate to upstairs but they must get a conviction for his murder. It is a small town, and I have a bad reputation. That is why I tell your kids about your brands; anything that you do, your brand speaks for you. Because my brand was not good—a hard head in the streets—my brand fits the description of a murder. I was capable of that at that time, and it could have been me at that time, but it was not. In any other circumstances, I could have gone that route. One thing the judge knew was that I would not do anything to anyone unless they did something to me because I was a protector more than anything else. All my acting up and fighting was because someone did something to me. I even carried that same attitude into the penitentiary.

Speed it up now to the trial; they spent 48 hours; no, I will give them 72 hours from my paperwork preparation for my case. So, to get that money for my case, they must put in what they did while working on my case. They said they did this and they did that, and most of what they put in was phone calls to me, a letter, things like that, and after I was convicted and locked up, I got my paperwork and saw they only spent 72 hours on my case, a murder case. That is all the time they have for my case, a case with the possibility of someone spending their whole life in prison. After going through my paperwork…they never found a gun. There was no motive, but still convicted me of murder.

So, first I was going back and forth to small hearings, and they always had me shackled up. The day of my trial I went in with no shackles on, and I thought I was going home that day. I thought this was it; this is about to be over, my little girlfriend in Norfolk; it's about to be over with it. So, that morning or the morning before we went in for trial, my lawyer came to me, and he said, "I got them, I got them." I gave you a plea bargain for three years. That didn't sound good to me at all because I know that I didn't do it. If I had anything to do with it and with the mindset that I had, the street codes that I lived under, and if I had anything to do with it, if I was with someone and we got caught up, I would take it; I would have taken those three years. So, when he said I got you a plea deal for three years, I said no, I will not admit to something I did not do.

SN: How can you give someone a plea deal of three years for a murder charge?

So, I declined it and said that I was not pleading guilty for something that I didn't do. I said that my mom told me to never plead guilty for something that you didn't do. He said something, trying to be smart; he said, "Your momma is not here."

I will never forget because I am in the holding cell, we're talking through the glass, and the other guys are in there, and now everybody knows that I'm locked up for something that I didn't do, a murder that I didn't do. So, at that time, other people had to go to trial that day, so we were all in the holding cell, and everybody's lawyers were coming up to the glass and telling them what was going to happen. So, everyone knows that Smoke is going home today and that I'm out there today; it's over for Smoke. So, I said no to the plea bargain, and my lawyer said they were going to give you 50 years. I looked at him and said, "I'm going to do it standing on my mother fucking head." The lawyer just said, "Alright!" They still think they had one more shot; they threw the bait out there, and I did not take it. Let's try one more thing. So, they got me and took me to another holding cell because now the other guys in the holding cell are mad. The guys are like, "What do you mean by plea bargain? Smoke didn't do it;

So, they took me to another holding cell, and now I'm sitting in there, and the door opens. It's my female lawyer jokes and my momma. So, we sat in there and started asking me questions, and I'm like, they brought my mom to try to make me take this plea bargain; they talked to her about it. Like telling my mom, you need to tell him to take this plea bargain. At this time, I had a little female I was messing with in Norfolk, and we didn't know if she was pregnant or not, so my mom's like, what if she's pregnant and you're not going to see your child? I said they will see me when I get home because I'm not taking a plea bargain for something I did not do. My mom was like, they are talking about the death penalty; they are talking about life. I said, Mom, I didn't kill that man, so they can talk about whatever they want to talk about, but I'm not pleading guilty because I didn't do it. My mother then looks at the lawyer with tears in her eyes and says, "He's not going to take the plea bargain." I'm 17 years old and willing to do 50 years. She kissed me, a tear dropping from my eye, and she said, "we are going to fight then." We go back in, and the trial starts. Shawn gets back up again and testifies like he doesn't even know me, dressed in his white shirt. In the beginning, he had locs; he cut his hair. So, we are sitting there, and he is telling his story. At the time, as he was talking, I was looking at Danny's family.

The Trial

So, after the lawyer told me what type of time I was looking at getting, they came to me with the plea bargain for three years, and the lawyer told me that I was going to get 50 years if I did not take this plea bargain.

So, the trial starts, and this trial felt different because every other time I had to go to court, I was in shackles. This time, when I went to Trial, they did not put shackles or that belt on me. So, I am thinking it is about to be over. I'm about to be free to go home because I'm not chained down like a slave. So, I am sitting there, and the Commonwealth starts calling their witnesses, so they call Shawn Coleman, and Shawn gets up on the stand and starts telling the story of how he does not know me again. I came from around the back of the building, shot the man, ran off, and then came back and shot him again. While he is talking, I am looking over at Danny's family, and I'm looking like I hope they can read my expression and feel my energy. I didn't do this as I am looking at the family.

　I am hearing what Shawn is saying, but I'm facing the family. I'm shaking my head at the stuff that he is saying. A lot of people there were between Petersburg and Hopewell and they knew me. One thing that happened while we were sitting there, where I was sitting, was that I was looking past my lawyer to look at the family. Then my lawyer said to me, do I want to see this picture—he was referring to the picture of Danny? I never saw this man in my life; I did not know the man, so my lawyer opened the folder and showed me his photo, and I said, I still don't know him. I'm looking, and I'm still like, I still don't know him. I never met this man, and they are accusing me of murdering a man that I never met a day in my life.

So, after Shawn gets off the stand, they call their second witness. After my lawyer cross-examined Shawn, he did well and crossed him up with some stuff about being a court-appointed lawyer, Ray Lupold. He made him say some stuff about how they knew Shawn was lying, which should have caused some reasonable doubt. After that, the next witness was the white man, Bobbie, a fifty-something-year-old man. He got up on the stand, and he was their powerful witness. He was the witness who said he was just checking his mileage (verify). They call him, and he takes the stand and begins to tell his story. He said that I had a bald head, but I had an Afro; I had no facial hair yet. So, the witness said that the person had a bald head with a full beard. So, I was listening, and it was crazy. At that time, I had cut my hair down and still had no facial hair.

As we are going through the trial, he's telling his story about how he looked up when he heard the pop. I'm just looking and listening. Now is the time for my lawyer to cross-examine him. Some of the things that Mr. Poner and Shawn said were just not adding up. They asked the witness if he picked the person out of a photo lineup, he said did it out of the photo lineup, and he said yes. So, they asked if you put any marks on the picture, and he said yes, I put an X on the picture. They pulled my picture out, and it has no marks on it. I was not the one he picked out of the lineup. But they kept pushing. One of the questions they asked Shawn was about the coat. So, when they came to Norfolk and got me, they took a picture of me with a Georgetown starter jacket on, and when they asked Shawn what he saw when I ran away, he said a blue coat. So, they showed Shawn the picture of me that they took! He says that I had on a blue coat, a hoodie, and the gun was up in my sleeve! Nobody saw the gun. They asked him if he saw me running away, and he said, "Yeah." They asked him if the jacket had anything on it, and he said, "Naw." They asked him, "Did you see the gun?" and he said no; the gun was up in his sleeve. They assessed the coat for gun powder residue, and there was none on it. So, if you have a gun up your sleeve, some type of residue will be on me. But the crazy part about it was that it wasn't my jacket, so I was a bit nervous about that also. I traded off jackets, so that made me nervous about the jacket because anything could have been on that jacket. They asked Shawn again, if the jacket had anything on it, and the lawyer pointed out that the sleeve of the jacket was blue and gray! The lawyer picked up the jacket and turned it around, and it had a big Georgetown bulldog on it. You can't miss the bulldog. So, all this is not adding up, but I'm still looking at the victim's family. So, they take a recess so my lawyer can call our witnesses.

SN: What I heard later after the trial was done was that Shawn went out

in the hallway and the victim's brother was there at the trial and he pushed up on Shawn and said, "Where is the guy who killed my brother Shawn?" Shawn said, "That's him in there," and the brother said, that kid did not kill my brother; he said you're lying, that kid that did not kill my brother, Shawn. Then Shawn ran and got away from where the victim's brother was.

So, we came back from recess and they started calling my witnesses, so first my lawyers, being court-appointed, tricked me. At the time of the crime, I was in a house full of people, and I had alibi witnesses. The lawyers did not call any of my witnesses—none of them. They did not call any of the witnesses; I told him to call on. Where the guy got shot was at a Breeze Inn gas station, right before you got to Fort Lee and all the new hotels that are there now; that's where he got killed. He was shot in broad daylight.

So, they called witnesses, at the time of the shooting Shawn was standing next to Danny and he was standing next to Norris Hardy. Norris came to court to testify for me; my lawyer called him. Norris said that he had never seen me before. Norris is standing right next to the man who got shot and that he had never seen me before. So, when Norris said he never saw anything, (How can two people standing next to each other see a man get killed and one says you did it and the other says he never saw you?)

SN: There was a lady who worked in the gas station as a cashier. How I found out about her being a witness to the murder was that her boyfriend ended up getting locked up in Hopewell City Jail. Her boyfriend says to me, "Smoke, you didn't kill that man." "My girlfriend Connie was working that day, and she saw the man running after the shots, around the side of the store." So, I'm in jail, and I'm thinking, OK, I'm good. Can you give me her number? So, I gave her name and number to my lawyer, so he called her, and she became a witness. She told my lawyer that I was not the one that she saw; he was not the person that I saw do it!

So, I know now there are two witnesses for me and two against me. So, it was split right down the middle! What I learned later about murder charges was… reasonable doubt. What they said in the OJ trial was, "If it doesn't fit, you must acquit." The prosecution had another card, but they didn't expose it. The reason they didn't expose it was because it would have worked in my favor.

SN: Remember earlier in the book when I said that when I was standing on the corner and Shawn was telling the story and he mentioned who was out there, he mentioned Keshia and her sister Wormy were out there, and I said if Keshia and Wormy were out there, they were going to tell what they saw.

They had witnesses which were Keshia and Wormy who ended up being Commonwealth witnesses, and they told the Commonwealth that I didn't do it. The Commonwealth had a list of witnesses they were going to call, but they didn't tell my lawyer about Keshia and Wormy so they weren't called and my lawyer couldn't cross-examine because it would have worked in my favor. So, we are going through testimony after testimony, trial, evidence, and nothing working, so at the end of the trial, when it's time to pass for judgment, the judge looks down and then he looks at me. He tilted his glasses, and he said, "this case is 50/50, and it could have gone either way." So, again, I think I'm about to go home. The judge is saying this case is 50/50, and I'm hearing reasonable doubt, and I'm thinking that's enough. Then the judge says, "But I find the defendant, Eugene Porter, guilty."

At that point, all I heard was guilt and then screaming. Everybody was screaming, and when I turned around, everyone had run out of the courtroom, except for Keisha and her mom, who were sitting in the back crying. As I was sitting there, realizing that my life was changing, one tear dropped from my eye. At that current moment, after the guilty verdict from the judge, I had to grow up at once. So, I wasn't given a sentence, and it was set for me to return to court the following month. So, when I left the courthouse, they put me back in shackles.

SN: Going back, they had called other witnesses, like the detectives, like Rose Camacho and Mike Woodson, who both testified that Mr. Piner told them a different story. The witnesses for me, like the police officers, are saying that it's not me.

So, when I got back to the jail, I made two phone calls. The first phone call, I called my mother, and I had told my mother one thing and I had her promise me one thing, I was like, Look, if I go up here and anybody tries some gay stuff, I am not coming home; I am not never coming home(meaning a life was going to be taken) and I made my mother promise me that she wouldn't die while I was in prison. I said to my mother, if you die while I'm in prison, I'm going to kill Shawn because I'm not going to have anything left. People would say, you have your sisters, but my sisters are just my sisters, and my mother is my mom. That's my mom; you see what I'm saying. My sisters can go on with their lives and do what they do, but your mom is your mom. The thing is I didn't put myself in this situation and I didn't commit the crime. I told her that, and my mom was like, "Ok, smoke, I'm not going to die, I'm going to be alright." Because at this time, I didn't know how much time I had. At that time, I couldn't even think about the time I could get and still could not contemplate this. My second phone call (back then we remembered phone calls—we made a code whether it spelled out a name or something to remember them)—I remembered Keshia number and I dialed it. They answered the phone and accepted the collect call. The first thing they said was, "Smokie, you didn't do it.!" I said I knew, and they said it again, "Smokie, you didn't do it." We told them you didn't do it, and they cried over the phone. So, now I'm in jail, and I can't cry.

SURVIVING

Fast forward I get into a couple of fights in jail, just trying to learn how to survive. This went on before I got my time.

SN: One more thing, and may he rest in peace. And everybody knows my street legend—my godbrother Mook. Mook held me down; he came to see me, and we were still thinking that I was getting released. I was feeling like this is the justice system, this must turn around.

I remember that I did not get many visits when I was in jail; my cousins Dominique and Michelle, my mother, and Mook came to see me. The day Mook came to see me, I will never forget that he had on the red NC state shirt—NC Wolfpack. His arm was wrapped in a wristband-ace band. Mook was getting it in those streets. Mook was sixteen at the time and as I'm looking at him through the glass window, and I'm like, what happened to you? He was like, man, dudes robbed me for $1200, but it will be alright. I was always on business stuff, so I was like, man, you got to get into some business stuff. He was like, when you come home, you are going to take care of all of that. He said I will have the money and you can take care of everything else, but at that time, I did not know that would be the last time that I would see him. Mook was killed by Hopewell Police. I have a tattoo that says Mook, RIP. Mook made sure I had commissary and my family was good.

Now it's time to go back to sentencing. The commonwealth is saying how much time they think I should get. They say life is in prison. So, I am like life, for something that I did not do. They had mentioned the death penalty one time because of how the man got killed, and when the commonwealth started saying that because of my history with the law and how I have been in a lot of trouble, he is a career criminal, and he deserves life, then Judge Lamon, says "as for the things that Mr. Porter has done as a juvenile, he doesn't deserve to spend the rest of his life in prison." Everything he did in his past was because of something that was done to him. So, they started bringing up stuff that I did.

SN: This is what I try to tell kids these days—your brand will follow you!

They brought up me punching someone in the face in school. They mentioned everything that I did, and once you get into the system, the first time you get a bad report in elementary school, it's all logged in. That's the prison pipeline.

SN: Everything you do, from elementary school on is preparing for the prison pipeline.

I used to do dumb stuff, like fights and all that, different dumb stuff, but everything that you do follows you through your life. Even when parents take their kids to see a psychiatrist, they are building up your pre-sentencing report. My pre-sentence report says life-life. I still have all my transcripts, which say life-and-death. But when the judge says Mr.

Porter has done something but nothing that deserves him to spend the rest of his life in prison, he does deserve a second chance after all of this! So, I'm like a second chance—wait a minute; I didn't get my first chance because I didn't do it! When the judge says, I'm going to give him 50 years—the same 50 years they already talked about—they already had a plan. The same 50 years that the lawyer came and told me about, if I didn't take the plea deal for three years, I was going to get 50 years. So, they gave me 50 years with twenty-five suspended! So, back then when you got sentenced, you had to do at least fifteen. The way sentencing was done at the time was different. Once I get to jail, I'm hearing numbers and computation. So, with 25 years I was supposed to do 5 years before I could be up for parole and the mandatory twelve.

To break it down, there were three laws back then in Virginia. You had the old law, which was you get thirty for thirty and get out. So, for every 30 days, you get 30 days. Then, when Douglas Wilder became our mayor, they were trying to get tough on crime, and he passed two-thirds of the laws for violent offenders. So, you must do two-thirds of your time back in 1993. Then, in 1995, they came out with no parole. So, no parole means if a person gets 20 years, they must do 18 years of the twenty. So, they made parole disappear, and I was supposed to fall under the old law 30-30. But when I got my first timesheet, it showed my time and accumulation of good time. So, all I know is that I am 25 years old. So, the guys that have been in prison are like, "Ok, smoke, you have 25 years; that's nothing—you do 5 years; you go up for parole, and you're going to make parole."

So, I'm like, I'm 17, getting ready to turn 18, so I'm counting 19, 20,... so I will be in my early 20s when I get home. Still, that gave me a little hope, and I'm like, I can do this even though it's not mine. I can do five, so I get to Southampton Receiving Center.

SN: My biggest thing is that I always wanted the McClure family to know that I didn't kill him.

Juvenile-Southampton

So, I get to receiving at Southampton receiving; it smells like cow poop; it stinks; you're in the cells; you are meeting people that you never met. A lot of the guys I was in contact with are still brothers now. I am in receiving, and you are in a two-man cell because I had to go to the juvenile prison. You must go to South Hampton, which is the gladiator school! We did not understand the cowbell in receiving, and we would hear the cow bell, and we asked what that sound was. The cow bell will ring every time somebody gets killed over there. So, you are nervous because you know that when that bell rang, somebody got killed.

So, my first job was a job in the kitchen. Sometimes dudes get trustee status while they are still in receiving, and they do not have to go to the other side of the prison. So, with me thinking that I only have five years and if I can do my five years in receiving, I am good. There is a little bit of stuff going on, but it's not like over there in the prison. So, one day I'm in the kitchen washing dishes because I have the dishwashing job in the kitchen. I'm washing dishes, and this big guy, Doc, comes over to me. He is looking at me, and I'm looking at him. He is looking at me, as I have my hand in this cleaning water. He was like, "Man, are you Smokie?" I am like, yeah, who are you? He is like, "I'm Doc, and I'm from Prince George." I was like, "Okay, what's up? and he started telling me how he knows my cousins, then he said, "Man, you're going to be alright, and I got a message for you from Bae," (who I later find out that she is Danny's girlfriend.), saying that they know that I didn't kill Danny. He says again, you are going to be alright. So, when I heard that, I was like, OK, they know that I didn't do it, so when I went back to my cell, that gave me a little bit of hope.

At least the family knows that I'm not the one who did it. So, I'm trying to stay in receiving, and I remember the day that they were about to put me on trustee status. The white guy, my supervisor, came to me and was like, Porter, we're going to put you in for trustee status. So, I'm happy, like, I don't have to go anywhere, and then later that same day, they said "Porter transfer." So, I was trying to get to the kitchen and talk to my supervisor; maybe he can stop it-he couldn't stop it! So, they drove us across the street in a bus, which goes to South Hampton Prison. When we got over to prison and all that stuff that was said about prison and how you are considered fresh meat-all that is true.

When we got over there, they walked us up this hill, and when you're walking up the hill, one of the buildings (C1) is facing towards us, so all the inmates are looking out the windows, and they are hollering fresh meat, those youngins. By that time, I was growing my hair back, and I had a little twist in my hair. I'm 5'6 by then, maybe 134 pounds, which is small. So, we are walking and we have to go to laundry first, so we walk into laundry and we get there they gave us these jeans with elastic in the back, so three pairs of jeans, three t-shirts, boxers, and socks—you get everything new first, and then we have to go to C-3, which is the SHU/Segregation and the top tier is where all the new inmates come. So, it's like receiving all over again. So, when I get there at this time, people can still wear their street clothes; they can order clothes and wear them. So, I'm sitting there, and one of the guys, one of the Spanish guys, had come before me to South Hampton, but we were cool! In the streets, I saw a few gay people, but this was my first time really seeing them and being in the same space with them, not really knowing what they were. I mean, one walked past my cell, and when the guy walked past, he had long hair, a purple shirt, and breasts. So, I called over to Tito, and he was like, "what up homie," and I said, do they have chichas in here? He was like, no Homie. That really threw me off; I thought I was in a co-ed prison and I was thinking this was going to be alright if we have females in here, I can do this! So, he said there were no women in here, but I know I just saw a woman; I'm not crazy. So, I'm like, I need to stay by the door and watch for it to walk past again. I know I hear female voices, but I can't see what I was hearing.

So now I'm standing on the gate, looking, and the dude walks back by, and I can see his face now, and I'm like, oh snap, that's a nigga, a man, my stomach started hurting.

SN: Before you get to any prison, your name goes before you! People already know who you are and your crime before

you   get   there.

When I was in detention, I had a crew that fought together, ate together, and did everything together. The young man who was with me had already gone to prison. O'Dawg had 63 years, and Luis had life. So, the first time I saw someone get stabbed, we were looking out of the TV room because they weren't really letting us mingle with the general population. I saw two dudes, a big one and a slim one, and they were in each other's faces. The small dude pulled out a shank and stabbed the big guy, and the guy who got stabbed took off running to medical. Then I heard that bell ringing, and I'm like, this is real—I witnessed someone getting stabbed in here. It's really getting scary, so I'm like, I got to get myself a knife. If this is the way it will be, I need a knife.

SN: I found out the two guys that I knew that came in before me ended up crossing over and getting tricked.

One of the guys ended up messing with the punk that I saw walk past me, O'Dawg looked up to the guy who started messing with the punk, so he followed him. So, the story I was told was that "L" got raped by these guys. "L" was in the cell and got caught up with the punk, and the punk boyfriend came in and was like you were messing with my boy, and now I'm messing with you. It was crazy, so they expected me and the punk's boyfriend to get into it because they knew me in the streets and that I could fight. Whenever it is known in the streets that you can fight, that will follow you everywhere that you go! We ended up talking, and I told him I wasn't into that.

Another of the biggest things that happened to me there was that my prayer life changed. I used to believe in God the way other people did—the traditional way. My mom made me go to church, and I ran from church. Early in my life, I became a Muslim, and I was praying five times a day. I was really into it! Once they tried me and convicted me for something that I didn't do, I felt that God had failed me. I felt that if no man knew I didn't do it, Allah knew I didn't kill him, and after they gave me 25 years, I didn't want to hear about God anymore. I could not understand how God was going to let me spend the rest of my life here. So, I ran from God and the traditions. Once I got put into the general population, I went to C-1, C-1 143, and everything changed. My name changed; you aren't Porter anymore; you are still Porter as the person, but you changed to the number 225345. I will never forget my number; you can never forget your number; I may forget my phone number, but never my state number. In fact, I had two numbers. There were so many people in prison at one time that they took away my old number and gave us all a new one, 1170747 was my new number.

I used to go in the TV room; now the TV

room is dangerous. The TV room in South Hampton especially around 10 o'clock with all those inmates in there at one time. People who are in South Hampton will tell you not to go into the TV room at 10 o'clock at night because if you have beef with anyone or anything, when that door in the TV room closes, it locks.

So, how I got into know more about being a Muslim, one night while I'm in the TV room, at that time I didn't know about the five percenters, so when I was in the TV room, I used to sit in the back on this bench and hear these guys talking, and it was like three or four of them. So, I used to stand on the outside of the stipend and listen. So, one of the guys said to me, "Why are you always standing on the outside? What are you seeking?" I said that I'm seeking knowledge. So, he asked me who I was, and at the time, I gave him my Muslim name, Kamille Ali Quan. He was like, okay, then I started being around five percenters (N.O.G) more. I can honestly say that when I became a five percenter, it changed my life. It made me not have to wait on a God that I could not see. I knew there was a god in me. There are levels to this, because if you didn't believe the five percenters, you were a savage. So, because I used to read all the time, I became an elder god at a young age. I did not read any fictional books during the first years that I was in prison. The first fictional book I read was when I went to the hole, and it was a book called *Lucky by Jackie Collins*. That was the very first fictional book I read, but other than that, I am reading books that gave me knowledge. I read Albert Einstein, and I read Malcom X. As I got deeper and all the people that I enlightened and gave knowledge to, I made all my students read Albert Einstein. Albert Einstein was so deep into his thoughts that I wanted to transfigure into that form. With Albert Einstein, little things didn't matter anymore. Albert Einstein was so deep in thought that the littlest thing, like tying his shoe, he forgot how to do. He would be so deep into his thoughts that a path that he walked all the time he would end up getting lost. He was crazy—he was out of his mind literally.

My first enlightener, the god powerful, gave me the attributes of supreme Ala, and he told me that I was omnipresent, omnipotent, and everywhere. So, as I grew into myself, I took my Muslim name and, with the supreme alphabet, broke it down. King Allah Master Islam, which I absolutely Love. Ali means the most high, and Quan means master of the universe. What Jesus says is, "Did not I say that you are gods, but you shall die like men?" He said we will do greater.

So, me becoming a five-percenter kind of helped me to not go crazy while I was there. It helped me because when I found out how much time I really had to do, those 5 years changed. I went to my counselor, Ms. Tann and I got the update sheet for my time; the sheet said 2012, and we were still in the 1990's. The world did not end in 2000; they said the world was ending, so I'm like, I'm going to die here. So, I said to Ms. Tann, this must be wrong, and at that time, I found out about the two-thirds law. So, I was not under the first law now but the second law, meaning I had to wait 12 years before I could start going up for parole. I was getting moved around, stayed on the rock in the early nineties.

When I lost God, the new god that I needed found me. I say that because I never had to engage in same-gender relationships. For some reason, the staff members were willing to help me. They were aware of my case; people from Petersburg and Hopewell were like, Bruh wasn't supposed to be here. I was one who walked differently—I walked by myself, even though I had a team of guys. It was so crazy that I didn't even have a treatment plan.

Once my counselor read my paperwork, she said, Gene, you are not supposed to be in here, boy. So, if you tell me to do something, I'm not going to want to do it. Most officers from that area, like Mr. Smith, the captain, and others, watched me grow up. When these officers see me now, they say, Boy, you were hardheaded as hell, but they also respect how I carried it because I was the one who showed them respect, but if they disrespected me, I was disrespectful. They saw me grow through childhood, and these officers became fathers to me. The women CO's there became mothers to me because I didn't get to see my family for about 10 years. At that time, my family members weren't coming to see me; they weren't visiting. People didn't even want to go into prisons, and what makes it worse is that I'm in here for a crime that I didn't even commit. I'm not getting any visitors, not really having phone calls, but, back to Mook, before he was killed, he made sure I had money on my books, my godmother would answer my phone calls whether he was there or not, and I had three-way jumping. Mook got killed in 1999 by the police when I was locked up.

MY world shifted when Mook got killed with everything I had going on at that time.

In 1998, I got my first officer; she showed interest in me, and that really helped me as far as my bid was concerned. It helped me, and it hurt me. I thought I was in love; I was just talking more than anything. If you tell any woman, whether it's in prison or someone outside, that you have 18 months, they will stick with you for about 18 months. They will give you a good 18 months, and after that, they will dip. They be like this nigga ain't coming home. So, Kim was her name, and my boys said I was crazy about her. She showed me attention, and that was the experience for me that led to my being kicked out of Southampton. They found out about me and my guys; we were called the South Hampton lovers. We used to want to get out of Southampton, which had a population of five hundred. It was the rock, and everything was happening there—death and other stuff. A people from the wall, there were so much fighting, territoriality—it was gangs, but about where you were from. Richmond, Petersburg, 757, DC, and guys from Petersburg and Tri-City sat together, and when something went down—that Petersburg wild crew—you wanted them with you. They say that these Petersburg guys are strong and crazy, and they will fight. Between us and Newport News, and my guys were down there from Newport News. You start to get a feel for the guys, where they are from and who to hang around and not hang around.

The day I got transferred, I was in the honor pod then, and they came over with a list, and they were all these dudes getting transferred, including my youngin, Slim. Slim came upstairs to me, and I was like man dudes getting transferred out of here. There was a transfer list and the first time I went downstairs to look at the list, my name wasn't on there. Slim was like, man, your name is on that list to get transferred. I said, man, my name is not on that list because I just came from down there, and my name was not on that list. So, I go back down there, and there my name is on the list.

Now it was time for us to be transferred-it was so terrible how they transferred us; usually they take you to Powhatan and then get you on another bus to get you where you are going. They did a swap; they took us straight from Southampton to Greenville. They told us the warden said that by 1 p.m., he wanted us off his complex. It took us straight to Greenville. This was a different experience because at that time, they had dudes from out of state there; the Warden was there; it was different. The cells were so much different from Southampton, one thing I noticed was the cells were bigger. One of the things I can say is that once I found the god in me, I never let prison do me. People look at me and say, you don't look like you spent 18 years in prison—I did, though. I did the time given but didn't let the time do me. So, it was like I never went to prison because I knew I wasn't supposed to be there.

SN: If you're doing things that's not right, study the law-learn the rules.

When I started my appeal process, my appeals kept getting denied. My first appeal got denied, and my lawyer was like, it's fine; we are going to file a Habeas. He forgot to put some information on the paperwork about the witnesses. The first thing I ever learned about law was Strickland vs. Washington. It's a two-prong case where you cannot argue a lawyer's defense. So, my lawyer not calling my witnesses, even though it would have helped me, was his choice to make. Then we did Habeas, and again, stuff was left off, and they said we should have put it on

the first appeal. By that time, I had a paid lawyer because I told my mom that I didn't want any more white lawyers on my case; I wanted a Black lawyer.
Same thing happened with my new lawyer.

SN: Getting in the system is easy but getting out of the system is hard.

So, I'm in this prison called Luneburg. It's going well because it's a dormitory. They say once you get to a dormitory, which means you are close to going home. I'm in the dormitory, and again, like they say, when you come to prison, everybody already knows why you're in there. So, we had a dude from Petersburg who worked in laundry. At every facility you go to, you must go to the laundry first. So, we went to lunch, and one of the guys was like, "Yo Smoke, there is another dude up here from Hopewell." I said, oh yeah, well, there can only be two people from Hopewell, and that's one of my little cousins, or the nigga who lied on me and it was Shawn. We were at lunch, and at that time they were just bringing Shawn in with his stuff for another case, but he didn't know what I looked like anymore. I will never forget his face, but he doesn't know what I looked like now. It had been 8 years since he saw me. So, I'm walking down the boulevard with my guys, and I looked and was like, Naw, it can't be. He is pushing his cart with an officer. So, I go to Chow, come back, and I'm sitting by the washing machine, and my homeboy Rock comes, and he knows Shawn too because they're all from Hopewell. I'm sitting there, and I have tears in my eyes, so my homeboy says, "Yo Smoke, what's up? Are you alright?" I said, man, I must kill him, and he was like, Smoke, what do you mean, man? You can't do that, bro." I said man, God, and the devil can't exist on the same planet. He was like, "Man, it must be a better way, Smoke. How am I supposed to explain that to your mom, your family, or either one of y'all families?" I said, man, he put me here. I was like, Naw man, he can't stay here. So, now everybody knows he's here, and they're trying to talk me out of it because I was waiting on an appeal at the time. So, they like you waiting on your appeal; you're going to get out, and if you do something to him, then you're never going home. So, I'm thinking and contemplating. So, we usually go to A-chow, and I needed to be in B-chow. I have a homeboy from Charlottesville there with me. I said, Yo, I need to go in B dining hall, bro, because dude up here. So, everybody knew about knew everything that was going on because they had been around me all the time. So, he was like, "Man, I'll go with you, Smoke." I was like, Alright, so we go in B-chow. I walk in B-chow, and Shawn is sitting at the table, and we pull up and sit down. We sit at the table, and I have the knife in my pocket. I looked at him and was like, yo, what are you going to do, man? "He was like Smoke; I know you didn't do it; I just don't want any trouble."

I was like, are you going to help me

get out? "He was like, Yeah, man, I'll help you, whatever I have to do, man." I was like, okay, are you going to talk to my lawyer?

SN: By this time, I had already started studying law.

All I need you to do is tell my lawyer that I didn't do it, and we will go to court, and you can plead the fifth after I get a new trial. I said, but I need you to go and say what you need to say to get me a new trial. "He said, man, I got you."

So me and Scrap leave, and I'm like, alright, I'm feeling refreshed now because here comes my chance to get out again. So, my mom and my middle sister Ta'Mika came to see me, and I was like, Yo, Shawn is up here. My sister said one of the most powerful things that she has ever said to me, and by that time she had-had my first niece. I told them that Shawn said he was going to tell my lawyer that it was not me—the truth. Tamika said, "Smokie, he already lied on you; don't let him lie to you." So, I'm like, ok that was powerful and made so much sense. I hear her but I'm thinking like, ain't no way this nigga going to lie now. So, I called my lawyer, and my lawyer never came to see Shawn. By that time, Shawn had gotten his time and he lied.

SN: *Oh yeah, at first Shawn said he didn't lie to me, and I sent the paperwork over to his dorm; he was in dorm one.*

I told my homeboys from Petersburg what happened, and they said, "What do you want to do, Smokie? You want to fight." I told the guys that Shawn could not have anything while he was here, so they took his TV and everything! It wasn't the fact that he snitched; it was the fact that he lied and got me in here.

Now, I'm thinking, how am I going to get this dude? So, my homeboys are like, you can fight him, and we can stomp him out. I was like, I don't want to fight because anybody can win the fight; he needs to go. I told them, "This is what I need you to do—all I need you to do is pick an argument with him on the boulevard; when you do that, I'm going to come by and act like I am breaking it up." So, I'm telling them what I am going to do, and when I break it up, I'm going to hit him with the knife. When I pull it out, it's going to be too late, and he's not going to know what happened. By that time, he's going to just clutch the spot, and then I'm going to walk off and dump it. They were like Smoke, ummmmm, man, I don't know.

I was like, forget it and I don't want to talk about it. If y'all niggas don't want to do it my way, I don't want to fight! But the universe and God were on it because my birthday came up, and by that I had stopped celebrating holidays in prison. The only thing I cared about was my birthday. I had talked to my sister early in the beginning of the month, and she said, "I got you a card, and I'm going to send it to you." So, I'm waiting and waiting; my birthday comes, and I don't get the card. My birthday came on that Friday, and I didn't get the card. So, I'm like, ok, then Monday comes, mail comes, and I didn't get the card. At that time, I was taking college classes, so I'm sitting in the foyer and an officer says something to me, and I'm mad about the dude being here and I can't get to him. I'm also mad about my sister not sending my birthday card.

So, before I knew it, I snapped on the officer and caught a threatening bodily harm charge, but after I threatened him, I was still able to go to class. Most of my charges were against officers, but when they came and locked me up and went in the hole- they found out that Shawn was up there. When I said everyone knew I was innocent, it was time for me to go to my hearing to get out of the hole, and the warden came to me, and he was like, Mr. Porter, I want to let you out of the hole, but Mr. Coleman is here. I don't know if it's going to be the safest thing to do. I was like, man, I ain't going to do anything to him. The warden said straight out of his mouth that, "if the person who lied on me and put me here, I would want to get them." So, he said, "I can't take that chance on you doing something to him while he's here." So, they ended up transferring me because of it, and I was like, I was here first!

But it's easier to transfer me because I was in the hole. So, I ended up being transferred, which in fact saved me from catching a real murder charge. I was already plotting and scheming; I already had the knife. As time went on, I bounced from prison to prison, learning how to be a man and really growing up in prison and everything that came with it. The year 2000 came and went, but it didn't kill us.

Statistics

There are many men (Black men) who have been wrongly convicted of a crime that they did not commit. Far too many times, as you see with the Mr. Porter story, all the evidence points in their direction, but justice must be served, but served wrongly. Below are some statistics that we researched so you can understand the magnitude of how many people are in prison for crimes they did not commit. Some are exonerated, and some, just like Mr. Porter, who claims his innocence years after being released from prison, have not been exonerated. The results are very shocking, and it happens too much to just ignore the issue. Eugene Porter- You just read his story, but here are a few more men who were wrongly convicted.

Here are some facts to know before reading the stories of these other innocent men who were wrongly convicted:

- Between 2% and 10% of convicted individuals in US prisons are innocent.
- 2,666 people have been exonerated in the US since 1989.
- Proven innocent people have served more than 23,950 years in prison so far.
- Out of one hundred sentenced to death, four are likely innocent, but only two get exonerated.
- Sixty-nine percent of wrongful conviction cases happen due to eyewitness misidentification.
- False confessions account for 29% of wrongful convictions.
- Official misconduct plays a part in 31% of murder exonerations.
- False accusations are present in 70% of wrongful convictions.

Wrongly Covicted

Arthur Lee Whitfield

On August 14, 1981, Arthur Lee Whitfield was accused of the rape of a woman in Norfolk, Virginia. Twenty-five years ago, the woman identified Whitfield as her attacker, describing him as a tall, muscular black, light skinned with hazel eyes (Washington). This description was also used to identify an attacker from another rape that occurred earlier that night. Whitfield was tried and convicted for these two rapes and sentenced to 63 years (Washington).Whitfield was released by Virginia authorities August 2004, when a Norfolk prosecutor said DNA evidence proved Whitfield did not commit the two rapes. Whitfield had already served 22 years for the rapes that DNA proved he did not commit (Innocence Project).

The woman in the alleged attack does not agree with the DNA testing, saying she knew who she saw. The victim questions state authorities on the profile of Mary Jane Burton, the former crime lab scientist whose work has sparked a review of hundreds of cases and exoneration from the former governor, Mark Warner (Isadora). Whitfield was released on parole, but is trying to get a pardon from the Virginia governor, Tim Kaine. Since the Virginia Supreme Court did not declare him innocent (Isadora), if Whitfield does not get his record cleared, he will be a registered sex offender for life.

Julius Ruffin

On December 6, 1981, Julius Ruffin was accused of raping, sodomizing, and robbing a woman in her home. The victim looked for a Black male and identified Ruffin as her attacker, though the description did not match up (Mid-Atlantic Innocence Project). Ruffin is 6'1" (187 cm), with light skin, and two distinguishable gold teeth and facial hair. She identified her attacker as 5'8" (174 cm) with dark skin. On October 1, 1982, he ended up being sentenced to life in prison.[1] In June 2002, Virginia courts passed a law that allowed felons to petition the courts for DNA testing. On February 13 of the following year Ruffin was released by DNA testing. Ruffin was pardoned by the former governor of Virginia and given $1.5 million in compensation (Innocence Project).

Earl Washington Jr. (born May 3, 1960) is a former Virginia death-row inmate, who was fully exonerated of murder charges against him in 2000. He had been wrongfully convicted and sentenced to death in 1984 for the 1982 rape and murder of Rebecca Lyn Williams in Culpeper, Virginia.[1] Washington has an IQ estimated at 69, which classifies him as intellectually disabled. He was coerced into confessing to the crime when arrested on an unrelated charge a year later. He narrowly escaped being executed in 1985 and 1994.

Washington was scheduled for execution in September 1985 but a *pro bono* defense effort and appeal gained a stay while working to gain appeal of his conviction. Based on questions about his murder conviction raised in 1993 due to DNA testing, which had not been available at the time of trial, Washington's death sentence was commuted in 1994 by Governor Douglas Wilder to life imprisonment. In 2000 additional DNA testing was done, as new technology was available. Based on this, Washington was pardoned by Governor James Gilmore and released from prison. In 2006, he was awarded a settlement from the estate of Agent Curtis R. Wilmore, who had coerced Washington's confession. In 2007, he received a settlement from the state.

Thomas Haynesworth (born March 21, 1965) is a resident of Richmond, Virginia, who served 27 years in state prison as a result of four wrongful convictions for crimes for which he was exonerated in 2011.

Haynesworth was arrested in Richmond at the age of 18 in 1984 after a woman identified him as her attacker. He was convicted of four violent rapes in the East End of the city. He was sentenced to a total of 84 years in prison. Haynesworth maintained his innocence throughout the years of incarceration. Based on DNA and other evidence, the crimes for which he was convicted are now believed to have been committed by a neighbor who resembled Haynesworth.

In 2009, new state laws and procedures allowed for DNA testing, which was not available in the 1980s. Semen collected from the first attack implicated the neighbor and ruled out Haynesworth. After reviewing this and other evidence, local prosecutors brought the case to the office of Virginia Attorney General Ken Cuccinelli, who began advocating for Haynesworth. His convictions in two of the cases were vacated, and he was released from prison on parole in March 2011. Haynesworth was fully exonerated in the remaining two cases in December 2011.

The case, which *The Washington Post* called "one of the state's most extraordinary legal cases",[11] used DNA testing and new state laws that allowed convicts to present new evidence in cases to prove innocence. The General Assembly passed a bill in 2012 to pay Haynesworth compensation for his wrongful convictions and lengthy incarceration, amounting to a total of $1 million in a lump sum payment, two types of annuities, and tuition at a community college. The legislators wanted to help him make his way in his life.

The Norfolk Four, four former United States Navy sailors: Joseph J. Dick Jr., Derek Tice, Danial Williams, and Eric C. Wilson, who were wrongfully convicted of the 1997 rape and murder of **Michelle Moore-Bosko** while they were stationed at Naval Station Norfolk. They each declared that they had made false confessions, and their convictions are considered highly controversial. A fifth man, Omar Ballard, confessed and pleaded guilty to the crime in 2000, insisting that he had acted alone. He had been in prison since 1998 because of violent attacks on two other women in 1997. He was the only one of the suspects whose DNA matched that collected at the crime scene, and whose confession was consistent with other forensic evidence.

Nearly ten years later, after the four recanted their confessions and entered years of appeals, they gained support for a clemency campaign and received conditional pardons in 2009 from then-Virginia Governor Tim Kaine. New exculpatory evidence was found after that and the Norfolk Four were exonerated in 2017, receiving absolute pardons by Virginia Governor Terry McAuliffe.[1] In December 2018, they received a combined settlement of $4.9 million from the City of Norfolk and $3.5 million from the Commonwealth of Virginia for their wrongful convictions.

These four were among a total of eight men whom the Norfolk Police indicted and initially prosecuted as suspects in what the prosecution said was a multiple offender crime. Three men, named by others from the four, were released and their charges dismissed, because of lack of evidence against them. Omar Ballard, a man who had an independent association with the Boskos, was the last arrested for this crime in March 1999 after it was found his DNA matched that at the crime scene, and was the only match made. He confessed in March and April 1999 and insisted that he committed the rape and murder of Moore-Bosko by himself, but the prosecution continued to press the theory of a group crime. In 2000, Ballard pleaded guilty and was sentenced to one hundred years in prison, fifty-nine of which were suspended by the court. Forensic evidence is consistent with his account that there were no other participants.[3]

Each of the Norfolk Four had confessed to the police about these crimes, but later recanted their confessions, saying they had been threatened and coerced by the Norfolk detectives, and their confessions were false. Williams and Dick pleaded guilty to rape and murder before trial, under threat of receiving the death penalty. Dick testified for the state in trials in 1999 and 2000 against the other two defendants. Each of their DNA was excluded from matching that collected in evidence from the scene. As there was virtually no physical evidence against them, Wilson and Tice were convicted by juries based on their confessions. With the plea deals and trial, Tice, Williams, and Dick, were convicted of both rape and capital murder, and were sentenced to one or more life-sentences without having the possibility of parole (LWOP). Wilson was acquitted of murder but convicted of rape; he was sentenced and served 8½ years in prison.

Article written about Gene porter by Lyne Carey on June 13, 2019.

In 1993 at the age of 17 Eugene Porter was convicted of murder. A crime to this day he says he did not commit.

He was advised to take a plea deal. Porter knew that saying yes to a plea deal would mean less time being in prison. However, this would also mean that Porter would have to plead guilty. He told his attorneys and loved ones "I am not going to plead guilty for something that I did not do. He was sentenced to 50 years at Southampton Correctional Center.

"I Lost God when I went to prison," Porter said. "I was mad at everyone for letting me down, especially the judicial system." Porter has no problem with admitting he was not the best-behaved kid but he had a good heart. He was young and had to grow up fast now being behind bars. It was a life experience that not everyone could handle. While Porter tried to get early parole, it was denied on more than one occasion. He chose to focus on bettering himself and preparing for the one day he would be released from prison. In February 2012 Porter was released from prison after serving 18 years. The now 36-year-old man was going home. While behind bars Porter earned his GED and was certified in four trades including mechanics, HVAC, commercial cleaning, and business administration along with thirty college credits. Having accomplished some major goals, it still did not take away the fear of how he would be perceived in society once released. "I thought about what people were going to say about me. Are they going to call me a murderer? Will I even get a job?" He noted. Once released Porter found himself with more support than he could imagine from family, friends, and people in the community. Porter talked about the simple things he missed while serving 18 years of his life in prison. Such as looking up at the stars at night, or how about something as simple as opening the refrigerator door. There were no more pagers, everyone now had cell phones. The grocery stores now had self-checkout lanes which completely took Porter by surprise. "I had to learn how to drive again and I'm still working on the cooking thing." He said while laughing. Porter experienced at an early age the power of forgiveness.

"I have forgiven those that have done me wrong. I hold nothing in my heart but love," he said.

When Porter reflects on the years, he spent in prison he can see God never left his side. Waking him up every day, protecting him, giving him strength, support and guidance through staff and inmates within the prison walls was truly God at work.

Porter became aware there was a need in the emporia community and discovered a way he could contribute and assist with promoting healthier lifestyles for all ages through educating and elevating individuals through health and wellness while shaping their mind, body, and spirit.

"It was an easy match," he said. "I love working out and I love helping people." With a few bumps along the way, Porter's perseverance paid off. In 2016 S.T.R.O.N.G Temple Fitness and Personal Training was established. When asked what does "strong" stand for in the name and how did it come about?

"God gave me the name and the meaning," Porter said. "I asked him what do you want me to call it? It was the right thing to do since it is God's business. I just work for the company." The word S.T.R.O.N.G in a strong temple means (standing together relying on God). I asked God what do you want me to call it?

"My goal was to create a training center not a gym and one that was affordable to all. Don't get me wrong, the YMCA is nice and I support what they do for our community. But the reality is, not everyone can afford the Y."

Porter is dedicated to investing in the youth in hopes to prevent them from the streets and away from crime. David Blackwell, a supporter, and client said "I have been a member since 2016 and when I heard Porter's story it was enough motivation for me to become a member of the training center and help support his cause. He is helping to keep our young people out of the streets shows that he genuinely cares and I like that he treats everyone the same."

Porter believes if you can work out with your neighbors you are one step closer to strengthening the community. He shares his story with whomever will listen not to gain empathy but to inspire and give others hope. Porter has had the privilege to have trained several individuals from the community who have taken those skills to play sports for Virginia University. Those same individuals come back from college during the summer to give back to porters and the community by assisting with summer programs held at the center. Such as children summer football and boxing camp to name a few. In addition to dieting and exercise the hope is to mold their character and outlook on life. "I love it here; we are a family. We support each other and push one another through the workout. It's accessible, affordable and a place for the community members to get to know each other." Said Sierra Johnson.

Now don't let Porter's big smile and easy-going spirit fool you, he doesn't accept excuses. The training center does offer a variety of convenient health and fitness options for the entire community. Including individual and group training, virtual training, and for those clients that are immobile proctor will come to you. The center is open Monday through Friday from 5 a.m. until 8 p.m. And for those who have a busy lifestyle there is also 24-hour access available. S.T.R.O.N.G. Temple Fitness is located on Halifax Street in Emporia.

A Note from The Author

Being in prison and serving time for a crime you didn't commit is rough even when you get free it's hard to erase those memories…

-Gene Porter

These are years that I cannot get back!!

Made in the USA
Middletown, DE
09 October 2024

62158658R00066